# THE
## GHOSTLY TALES
### OF

# CHEYENNE

Published by Arcadia Children's Books
A Division of Arcadia Publishing
Charleston, SC
www.arcadiapublishing.com

Spooky America is a trademark of Arcadia Publishing, Inc.

First published 2022

Manufactured in the United States

ISBN 978-1-4671-9872-1

Library of Congress Control Number: 2022932236

All images used courtesy of Shutterstock.com.

# Spooky America

# THE GHOSTLY TALES OF CHEYENNE

## MARY KAY CARSON

Adapted from *Haunted Cheyenne* by Jill Pope

arcadia®
CHILDREN'S BOOKS

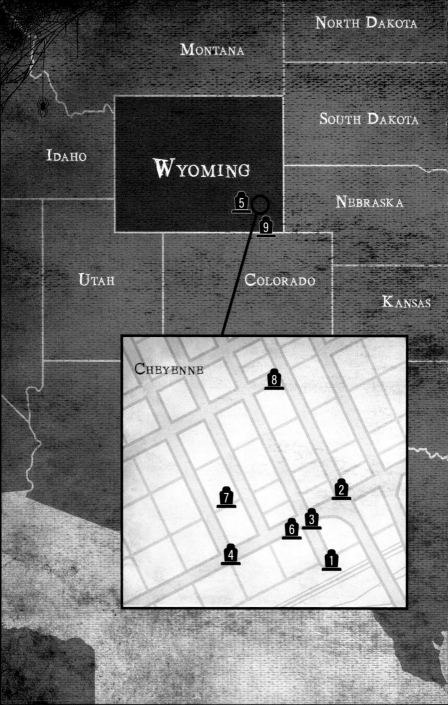

## TABLE OF CONTENTS & MAP KEY

# Introduction

Wyoming's capital city of Cheyenne (*SHY-an*) is older than the state itself. Union Pacific Railroad founded the Dakota Territory city in 1867, naming it after the indigenous Cheyenne people. The railroad giant wanted a train terminal along what became the first railroad to connect the east and west coasts of the United States. The promise of a transcontinental railroad connecting New York to California brought thousands of workers, shopkeepers, former American Civil War soldiers, and immigrants into Cheyenne. The first train arrived only a day after the tracks were laid. The town grew so fast it earned its nickname, "Magic City of the Plains."

Honest folk weren't the only ones hightailing it to Cheyenne in those days. Cattle rustlers, conmen, and thieves also smelled opportunity in the boomtown. In the late 1800s, Cheyenne was a true rootin'-tootin' Wild West town. It was a lawless place preyed upon by outlaws and patrolled by shoot-first-and-ask-questions-later vigilantes.

When Wyoming reached statehood in 1890, Cheyenne became its capital. Today, it's the largest city in Wyoming but continues to embrace its Old West roots. There's no better proof of it than Cheyenne Frontier Days, an annual ten-day summer festival that features the world's largest outdoor rodeo. In fact, the city is considered America's rodeo *and* railroad capital. Visitors can see bull riding as well as the world's biggest steam engine. Western-themed fun is everywhere, from dude ranches and train museums to shops specializing in cowboy hat/boot fittings and horse saddles of every sort. Yeehaw!

Century-old churches, theaters, and mansions help pass along Cheyenne's colorful Old West history from one generation to the next. According to locals, some of these historic places also harbor the spirits of those who once lived—and died—there. Many of the town's spookiest ghost stories are rooted in true tales of unfortunate railroad accidents, revenge-seeking cowboys, jealous lovers, and tragic disasters. After all, the most hair-raising ghost stories are those with enough truth to them to seem perfectly possible.

Cheyenne Depot Museum

# Tragic Tales from the Tracks

During the 1860s, the race was on to connect the Eastern and Western United States by train. One team of workers started laying railroad track in California and fought its way east. Union Pacific Railroad laborers began near Omaha, Nebraska, and worked westward. In 1869, the two would meet in Utah, connecting America's coasts and opening up the West. A journey that once took months by wagon was now only a few days by train. Building railroad tracks was exhausting, dirty, dangerous work. Hundreds died while blasting through mountains in landslides and from other accidents and disease.

Rail workers lived along the tracks, and temporary tent towns sprouted up as track was laid. Entrepreneurs and shopkeepers set up makeshift saloons, serving whiskey and games of chance to rail workers. Others sold food and essentials, including weapons. These grimy, crude, short-lived settlements moved along with the worksite, simply packing up and riding railcars to the next stop.

Cheyenne started out as one of these rough-and-rowdy places. Wyoming wasn't yet a state in 1867 when Union Pacific rail workers first set up tents near today's Cheyenne Depot Museum. The national historic landmark was built in 1886 by the Union Pacific Railroad, the largest train depot (station) in the West at the time. Made of beige- and brick-colored sandstone brought from Colorado and built in a fancy architectural style, the depot features a tall steepled clock tower and pretty arches. It became a museum in the 1990s.

Standing in the huge lobby on marble floors, it's easy to imagine long-ago travelers passing through or dining at the station's fine restaurant. After all, it's where the writer Ernest Hemingway celebrated his marriage to Martha Gelhorn. But like most transportation hubs, unhappy events also occurred there. There are documented horrific accidental deaths at the Cheyenne Depot, including a newspaper account of a rail yard watchman run over by a train in 1910 that left only mangled remains. Murders, as well, happened on site over the station's long history. Could these tragedies be behind the claims that ghosts haunt the historic depot?

Two years after the fatal train accident, another dead watchman was found only seventy feet away. A train hadn't killed this Union Pacific employee, however. A bullet ended the life of twenty-nine-year-old L.J. Sparr. He'd been fatally shot at close range. Armed watchmen patrolled the rail yard for thieves. Sparr's killer stole his gun but didn't take his wallet. So if it wasn't a robbery, what was the murderer's motive? Had a penniless traveler been caught trying to steal a ride on a freight car? Had they fought?

Watchman Sparr was known as a quick draw with a gun and someone always on the lookout for suspicious characters. His old job at the state prison gave him plenty of experience with dangerous criminals. Besides, a train conductor said he'd seen a stranger walking with Sparr alongside his train around midnight. It seemed likely that the watchman's murderer wasn't a random thief or train jumper but someone who knew L.J. Sparr personally—and had sought revenge. Three weeks later, Charles Taylor, who served time at the state prison when Sparr worked there, confessed to the crime.

Other murders that happened at the Cheyenne Depot were committed by those who spent the most time there—employees. A particularly odd coincidence of workplace violence involved Charles Bernard. A man was murdered on Union Pacific superintendent

Bernard's very first day in 1933. A recently fired clerk burst into the rail yard shop with a gun. Keith Bellars intended to kill the manager who'd given him the boot that Friday the thirteenth. Not finding him, the madman instead fatally shot another employee. Four years later, superintendent Bernard himself was shot dead by an unhappy employee who'd been fired for drinking alcohol at work. Perry Carroll turned his pistol on himself afterward but survived. He was executed in a gas chamber on Friday the thirteenth, dying with a smile on his face.

Paranormal experts claim that violent, traumatic events can create hauntings. If that's the case, the historic Cheyenne Depot Museum surely qualifies as ghost territory. Many people report seeing shadowy figures, hearing doors slam, and noticing items moved after hours when visitors are gone, doors are locked, and security alarms armed.

Lindsey, an event coordinator at the museum, feels that the place comes alive at night, like a station of traveling spirits. Long after closing time, she and her husband have heard giggling in the lobby and unexplained crashing sounds. They've seen glass doors opening and closing on their own and the dark figure of a woman. Others have watched earrings fly off the shelf in the gift shop, suddenly smelled the tar-like scent of creosote-covered railroad ties, and felt an invisible shove while descending stairs.

When members of the Paranormal Hunting Observation Group (PHOG) investigated the museum, they experienced events they couldn't explain. What kind of events, you

might ask? How about a light shining through a hatchway where luggage trunks were pulled up to a storage area. The group never found the light's source. There were no overhead light fixtures upstairs and no combination or positioning of flashlights could reproduce what they'd seen.

Dirt floors, old seeping rock walls, and cobwebs make most old basements spooky places. Some Cheyenne Depot Museum staff members won't go down into the building's century-plus-old basement—or at least not alone. Reports of scary noises, shifting items, and a reappearing white misty figure keep the faint-hearted away. When some teenagers asked to tour the basement, Andy, a man who works at the museum, obliged. As the group wound their way through a narrow, dim hallway underneath the depot, the last boy in the group shrieked. A rock had struck the back of his head. But there was no one behind him.

On a different evening, Andy was in the basement elevator with another man after the museum closed. They were going up toward the first floor when the strong tar-like stench of creosote filled the elevator as it lurched to a stop. Stuck between floors, the men yelled out for help. Finally they made enough noise to alert someone from the attached restaurant who came to their aid. No one else was in the museum at the time. The reason for the malfunction remains unknown. Just like the fate of many of those who passed through the Cheyenne Station for nearly ten decades.

# A Plainly Haunted Hotel

The railroad wasn't the only early transcontinental transport system to pass through Cheyenne. Once Americans began driving "horseless carriages," or automobiles, the nation needed a highway that connected the coasts. The Lincoln Highway was one of the first. In 1913, it stretched 3,389 miles (5,454 kilometers) from New York City to San Francisco.

The Lincoln Highway went right through Cheyenne along Sixteenth Street. Over the years, more modern highways replaced the Lincoln Highway, and Interstate 80 goes coast to coast roughly along the same route today. The section of the old highway in downtown Cheyenne came to be called Lincolnway, though some old timers still call it Sixteenth Street.

Hotels sprouted up along the Lincoln Highway, and none was finer than the Plains Hotel. Built in 1911 on Lincolnway Street near the train depot, more than a century of travelers have sought rest and comfort within  the "Grand Ole Lady of the Plains." Presidents, cattle barons, and movie stars entered the lobby striding beneath an ornate dome of colorful stained glass. They dined and slept in fancy rooms with plush carpet and velvet-curtained windows. Thomas Edison once demonstrated his phonograph machine in the Plains Hotel tea room. How astounded guests must have been to hear sounds coming from the early record player as they watched a flat, grooved disc turn underneath a needle. The hotel also was Cheyenne's first building to have telephones installed during construction.

The five-story pale-yellow-brick hotel remains a historic landmark and a working hotel with 130 guest rooms. The Plains Hotel is a favorite destination for fans of the paranormal seeking encounters with spirits. The hotel is said to be chock full of them, with ghost sightings reported on every floor—especially the fourth. A common story with many versions says someone fell from a fourth-floor window years ago. Accounts claim a young man was pushed, or perhaps jumped, to his untimely death. Guests staying in rooms on the fourth floor have reported smelling cigar smoke, the furniture unexplainedly moving, doors that lock themselves, and appliances that turn off and on.

Staff and guests of the hotel regularly see the spirit of a young blond boy around the age of eight. He shows up in the basement as well as near the grand piano in the lobby. Dressed in a white shirt, dark short pants, and white socks up to his knees, the blond youngster sports a Dutch-boy haircut (bangs and longish sides cut straight) popular in the early 1900s. Hotel staff sometimes shush the ghost when he noisily plays in the hotel lobby. No one's sure who the boy was, but there are two stories of boys dying at the hotel. One recounts a plumber's son who'd tagged along on a job in the hotel's basement. A loose pipe swung down and fatally hit the boy. Another tale says a child fell down the narrow elevator-like dumbwaiter shaft from the cursed fourth floor. Dumbwaiters carried trays of food, laundry, and other items between floors.

Murders and suicides have also happened at the Plains Hotel over its many decades. A 1924 article in the *Wyoming State Leader* reported on the sad death of Fern Blaylock, a former model and wealthy socialite from Denver who

divorced a cruel husband. She sued the Casper, Wyoming, oilman over land and was staying at the Plains Hotel awaiting a decision. People across the street noticed Blaylock sitting at an open fifth-floor window for some time. Bystanders witnessed her moving out onto the window ledge and then dangling from it. Her grip soon gave way, and the 43-year-old woman fell to the sidewalk and died. In her room was a quickly written suicide note. The medical examiner said Blaylock had taken a sleep medicine sold at pharmacies. The newspaper cruelly wrote, "She dropped to her death from the fifth-floor window, lured from the tantalizing hallucinations of drugs."

Many happy couples have celebrated engagements, weddings, and anniversaries at the Plains Hotel. However, a wedding night long ago instead ended in triple tragedy. The newlyweds had settled into the second-floor honeymoon suite after an afternoon ceremony of exchanging vows. Claiming to desire a drink of whiskey and a cigar, the groom left the suite. After what seemed like too long, bride Rose went looking for her new husband. Sounds of the orchestra playing floated up to the mezzanine. Peering over the balcony overlooking the lobby, Rose searched the merrymakers below. Shock struck her as she spied the groom flirting with a woman in a red dress. When she saw the cheating pair go into a private hotel room, Rose's broken heart turned cold with anger.

"So be it," thought the young bride. *Until death do us part.*

Rose fetched her husband's gun, went to the room they'd entered, and shot dead the groom and his red-dressed date. Then Rose returned to the second-floor honeymoon suite and shot herself.

To this day, wailing and crying are heard within the second-floor room where Rose retrieved the gun. But when the door is opened, no one is there. The spirits of all three who died that night have been spotted within hotel walls. A ghost, thought to be Rose, in a long blue gown is said to haunt the second floor. The spirit of a woman dressed in red and lace, as well. From the fifth floor to the basement, people have claimed to see a man dressed in an old-fashioned long-tail black wedding suit. A wedding-night double murder suicide apparently disturbs many souls!

Perhaps even stranger is a recent happening. Staff had decorated the Plains Hotel lobby for Halloween, including a spooky scene of mannequins dressed as bride and groom. The person working the front desk looked up at the balcony overlooking the lobby. She claimed to see the spirit in a red and lace dress looking down at the fake wedding scene. In the same moment, the bride mannequin toppled over. When the desk attendant looked back up at the balcony, the spirit was gone.

# CHAPTER 3

# Eternal Cowboys

Considered the "Daddy of 'Em All," visitors flock to Cheyenne Frontier Days every July to experience the world's largest outdoor rodeo and festival. It started way back in 1897 as a two-day rodeo and has grown bigger ever since. Today's Frontier Days celebration has rip-roaring fun for everyone. Besides the nine rodeos there are parades, concerts by country music's biggest stars, pancake breakfasts, chuckwagon cook-offs, and a famous Western art show. A lit-up carnival midway stays open until midnight and features thrill rides that spin, drop, twirl, and twist. Visitors get a festival-wide view from atop the Ferris wheel before testing their skills at the many prize-winning games along with midway. The rodeo events are the heart of Cheyenne Frontier Days. Competitors win more than $1 million in prize money each year doing everything from bull and bronc riding to steer wrestling and team roping.

Visitors to the festival should really complete their Old West look with a new pair of boots and a hat. There are plenty of cowboy outfitters in town. In fact, Cheyenne is cowboy culture central—and has been since its rough and rowdy beginning. Back before ranchers put up fences, cattle grazed on the open prairies.

When selling time came, cowboys simply rounded the cattle up and herded them to market. Left unprotected most of the time, cattle theft, or rustling, became a big problem. While ranchers usually branded their cattle stock with identifiable symbols, that only

helped if the thieves were caught. To deal with rampant cattle rustling, a group of riled-up ranchers created the Wyoming Stock Grower's Association in 1872. The group hired cattle detectives to secretly check the brands and thwart thieves. The legendary and infamous Tom Horn was one such cattle cop.

Horn headed west and joined the US Cavalry as a teenager. After a decade of respected service as soldier and scout, he spent his earnings building a ranch with one hundred cattle and twenty-six horses in Arizona. Not long after, rustlers stormed the ranch at night and stole all Horn's livestock. The theft turned Horn into a hate-filled hired gun willing to kill any man suspected of stealing cattle—or for the right price, some claimed. As a signature to his murders, Horn placed a small rock under his dead victim's head. During Horn's time on the Wyoming Stock Association payroll, fourteen-year-old Willie Nickell was found murdered near the gate of his family's sheep ranch and homestead. Under the teen's head was a small rock.

Horn was convicted of the boy's murder and sentenced to hanging. Some thought that Horn had been trying to shoot Kels Nickell, Willie's father. The teenager was killed wearing his father's hat and coat and standing beside the elder Nickell's horse. Still to this day, though, many believe that Tom Horn was actually framed. Regardless, he became the last person to be legally hanged in Wyoming in 1903. Horn was hanged in public, a gruesome punishment meant to shame the convicted and warn onlookers to abide by the law. Some say this dishonorable end left his spirit wandering.

The building that housed the US Marshal's office where Horn was interrogated still stands. Tales of spirit activity in the building are common and have been investigated by a paranormal team. An office worker often sees a transparent-looking man in a cowboy hat. She says he tips his ten-gallon hat like a gentlemen and then walks on.

Cowboy ghosts have a number of notorious Cheyenne haunts. A guest dining at the Plains Hotel noticed that her fellow diner's face had

turned to stone. Worried for her health, she grabbed her friend's arm. "Are you OK?" The pale woman replied with her own question. Hadn't she seen the translucent cowboy that just strode past them? She'd been able to see right through him. Overnight guests have reported waking up to find a cowboy sitting on their bed who quickly vanishes when looked upon.

The town's Wrangler Store is in a building constructed in 1882 that was once a bank and a hotel. The huge, three-story, red-painted brick building takes up a city block. Inside is more

than ten thousand square feet of ranchwear and Western clothing, such as hats, boots, and other accessories. The sky-lit hat room has hundreds of cowboy hats to choose from including a $1,200 diamond-studded Stetson. You can get a personalized boot fitting or have a favorite hat steam cleaned, too. Employees claim there's a cowboy ghost that comes up from the basement and wanders around the store. It rudely whistles at women who venture into the basement. Some of the staff have seen a form flee through the store, something nonhuman in shape.

Bert Pierce was another cowboy whose untimely death may have left his spirit in limbo. Pierce left Illinois at twenty-one to follow his dream of a life on the open range. He landed a cowhand job at Bard Ranch in 1912. After only a few weeks in the saddle, a freak accident took his life.

The Bard Ranch was east of Cheyenne, but the Bard home was in town near Holliday Park. Pierce was leading a horse from the ranch to the Bard home, walking beside the animal while holding onto its lead rope. Deciding to light a cigarette, Pierce tied the lead rope to himself to free up both hands. While still

attached by the rope, the horse suddenly bolted. Something—a noise, the smell of a match, a ghost?—had spooked the animal. It took off down the street, dragging Piece for several blocks, eventually hurling him against a telephone pole. The force of the impact and speed of the horse left Pierce unconscious and covered in bruises. The young man's skull had been fractured and his scalp torn loose. Bert Pierce died of his injuries.

Two brothers who rent a home across the street from Holliday Park believe it's haunted with a mischievous spirit. Could it be Bert Pierce? The tenants say they hear whistling when no one is there as well as boot stomping. Doors also swing open for no reason. At the brothers request, their pastor came and blessed the house. The unexplainable events calmed down some afterward, but still continue.

# CHAPTER 4

# Disasters of Long Ago

Cheyenne started out as a cluster of tents and ramshackle shacks along newly laid railroad tracks. The town grew with time, and people came to stay, constructing homes, stores, and buildings of a more permanent nature. But sometimes corners were cut. Safety was set aside for speed, defective materials and cheap labor unwisely chosen. Modern cities have rules and regulations about construction, but building and fire codes didn't exist in the nineteenth-century Wild West. Fires spread from a single home to entire neighborhoods, roofs caved in, and entire buildings toppled over.

Only three years after Cheyenne was founded and H.M. Hook elected its first mayor, the small city in the Dakota Territory nearly burned to the ground. On January 11, 1870, a fire began in a liquor store around eleven thirty in the morning. The *Cheyenne Leader* newspaper stated "a defective flue" (clogged

stove pipe or problem chimney) started the blaze. Strong prairie winds fanned the flames, and soon both sides of the downtown streets were burning. Business owners rushed into the buildings ahead of the flames' path to save what they could. Neighbors came to help, trying to put out the fires. But the rows of closely spaced wooden buildings didn't stand a chance.

The "Great Disaster," as the 1870 fire came to be called, destroyed eighty eight buildings. Two entire city blocks turned into a pile of smoking timbers and ash. The section of downtown lost was Cheyenne's busiest, a hub of entertainment. Saloons, pay-to-enter sideshows, and variety theaters competed with each other to separate cowboys and rail workers from their hard-earned pay.

Perhaps the most infamous was McDaniel's Theatre. Every evening at eight o'clock, a band started playing music in the street outside the theater's entrance to draw in crowds. Once inside, customers delighted in the carnival-like atmosphere. The owner, James McDaniel, knew how to sell tickets and was a true showman. A saloon sold refreshments, and a museum of sorts offered paying customers the chance to see monkeys, anacondas, and a grizzly bear. The theater itself offered a wide variety of entertainment. It staged some operas and Shakespeare plays, but sideshow acts attracted many of its visitors. Advertisements claimed audiences could see a real mermaid of the sea. A seven-foot-tall, four-hundred-pound English woman and a fifty-pound adult with dwarfism were among the other unusual performances featured at McDaniel's Theatre.

Downtown Cheyenne rebuilt after the Great Disaster fire and inspired many to construct buildings of brick and stone rather than wood.

Echoes of the fire seem to remain in a number of the shops that now occupy the sites where so many businesses burned long ago. The claims of ghost encounters are many, as is the reoccurring and unaccountable smell of smoke or burning within the buildings. Wendy, a boutique owner on the block, often smelled burning and a lingering smoke odor. Neither she nor the building's landlord could ever find its source.

Wendy also experienced strange happenings in the building's basement. One night after closing the shop, she was preparing packages for mailing in a lit section of the basement. Wendy said a woman's unsteady voice called out "Hello" from the dark end of the basement. The owner was sure she'd locked the doors but ran upstairs anyways to see if someone was there. No one was. A bit spooked, Wendy returned to the basement to finish up her packages. Before long, the voice once again called to her from the darkness. Deciding she'd had enough, Wendy sprinted up the stairs and left the store. After the encounter, she only used the basement during the daytime and often kept a radio blaring.

Linda, who owns a nearby antique store, also reports regularly smelling smoke fumes that have no source. She's seen spirits in her store as well, though she thinks it's likely that the antiques explain their presence more than the Great Disaster fire. Linda says one afternoon she greeted a woman wearing an old-fashioned Victorian outfit in her shop. Wanting her employee to see the wonderful costume, too, Linda called her over. The Victorian woman vanished. The next time a visitor from beyond stopped in, Linda had no trouble identifying it as specter. A man in a long coat stood only feet from the shop counter, but she could see through the gray particles that formed his translucent shape.

Not many years after the Great Disaster fire, another terrible tragedy happened. In September 1879, two downtown buildings— both constructed only four years earlier— completely collapsed. An earthquake didn't tumble them, nor a flood. Poorly mortared walls of inferior bricks doomed those inside the rooms above a music store and meat market. It happened at nearly ten o'clock at night, after the rooms' boarders were settled in for the evening. Cheyenne's residents heard a thundering crash, and many wandered out into the dark streets to search for its source as the fire alarm sounded.

Lit only by the pale moon was an unbelievable scene. Two entire buildings had been transformed into a piles of bricks, splintered wood, and dirt. Cries for help came from the heap, rescuers dug frantically, fires broke out, and people pulled neighbors from the rubble. Fifteen peopled plummeted to the ground along with the buildings. By one o'clock all had been accounted for except for two boys. At three o'clock, rescuers found the bodies of six-year-old Gussie and four-year-old Frankie. The brothers died together in bed with their arms around each other. Their anguished mother cried, saying she hadn't kissed her sons goodnight.

In 1887, eight years after the tragic collapse, the Atlas Theatre building went up on the site. Sightings of a boy specter playing with a red ball have been reported both in the theater and in the Wyoming Business Council building across the alley. Employees there claim to hear a ball bouncing on the floor, as if being dribbled, when no one is there.

By the 1930s, Wyoming was in its fifth decade of statehood and Cheyenne its capital city. Fire departments rushed to blazes, in shiny trucks to snuff out blazes and buildings grew taller and safer. But disasters come in all kinds, and sometimes their causes are never fully understood. At nearly midnight on June 27, 1934, a deafening explosion tore through three downtown buildings, and the blast echoed miles away. Bricks flew through the air, and people walking by found themselves suddenly sprawled out in the street. Most of those inside the buildings survived by struggling out of the rubble and fire that resulted. At least three women died, however.

At the blast's center was a grocery store with a rented room for boarders above it. A leaking natural gas pipe is the likely cause of the explosion, though investigators never found a leak. Firefighters recovered the bodies of three women—Doris Reed, Yvonne Signor, and Margaret Mitchell, who ran the upstairs boardinghouse. Two men were supposedly staying at the boardinghouse when the blast hit, but their bodies were never found.

A woman named Jodie claims to often see an apparition of a man while working on the same block as the 1934 explosion. He wears wingtip shoes, fashionable in the 1930s, and hides in

the shadows. Others who work there report an icy presence, a feeling of being watched, and a gate at the top of basement stairs that unlatches itself. Could it be the spirit of one of the lost men? Perhaps. A psychic once visited the dark, dirt-walled basement. She claimed all the spirit wanted was for people to use his correct name—Clarence—when encountering him.

# Haunted Homes

One should expect a variety of answers when asking the opinion of those who live in century-old houses. Do they like it? Some say no, complaining about the endless repairs to drafty windows, cracked walls, and gross basements. Other people love living in places with a sense of history and gush about original wood floors, plaster walls, and decorative fireplaces. One thing nearly all old-house dwellers have in common is the mystery of previous residents and their long-ago guests. Can anyone really be sure who slept in that bedroom a hundred years ago? Did someone jump out of a high window in decades past? What likely lies beneath that ancient floor in the cellar?

Ghosts and old houses go together, and Cheyenne has its share of both. One such house belongs to Candi and Charlie. The home itself has an interesting history. It's a prefab. A prefabricated house is manufactured in sections somewhere else and then shipped to its assembly site. The original owners of this house purchased it in Chicago in the early 1900s. The house arrived via the Union Pacific Railroad in sections. Originally assembled downtown, its owner moved the house in 1978. To save it from being torn down, Candi and Charlie purchased it and moved it a second time. Strange happenings started up even before the new owners had the house on solid ground.

The couple videotaped the unusual event of moving an entire house, but when Candi put the recording into the VCR, it was blank. Once the structure was in place and ready for furniture, the seven-year-old son told his parents he didn't want to live there.

Why?

"Because of the gray man in the window waving the lantern!" he said.

The family did move into the large yellow house, however, soon realizing that some of the spirits of those who'd once lived there had never left.

The gray man made another appearance to a brother-in-law spending the night. The guest woke up suddenly in the middle of the night, feeling as if someone else was in the room.

Opening his eyes, he saw a gray man seated at the foot of his bed. Then the ghostly figure rose up, drifted to the dresser, and looked as if he was setting some object down on top of it before vanishing. However, no one found anything on the dresser.

Voices of laughing children, as well as a man and woman arguing, have been heard more than once in the home without explanation— and family members find doors and windows open for no reason. Even the household dogs sense the spirits. They often tilt their heads, bark, and stare at an area where nothing can

be seen, especially the staircase, as if a ghost is going up or down the steps.

The bathroom seems to be an especially busy area of paranormal activity. One evening, Candi heard her youngest son screaming from the shower and ran upstairs to investigate. The boy blamed his brothers for rattling the doorknob and trying to frighten him. But both brothers were downstairs with their dad in front of the television at the time. Candi herself claims to have seen and experienced strange phenomena in the bathroom. Once she saw bathtub water splashing up on its own, and another time, she felt a hand touch her back while getting dressed.

The most upsetting ghost sighting happened when Candi and Charlie's son was in his final year of high school. A car full of teenagers pulled into the driveway. They'd come to take the son to a fun school event. The teens reported hearing a noise while waiting in the car and looking up through the sunroof to find its cause. Above the car, they saw a woman with long golden hair looking back at them as she floated overhead. The frightened friends bolted from the car and ran screaming into the house.

The Fort Russell house is another moved home that seems to have transported remnants of past residents with it. The house is one of dozens of wooden buildings that were built at the army camp in the nineteenth century. Fort D.A. Russell predates the city of Cheyenne. It was an early tent camp that became a permanent post in 1885. When the fort began replacing wooden buildings with brick ones, the city moved many of the structures into town. Teams of horses and steam-engine-powered tractors hauled homes on flatbed wagons from the fort to new sites in the early 1900s.

In 1976, a woman named Anna rented the house for her and her family. The home's owner and landlord told Anna that the house was haunted, but she dismissed the warnings and quickly moved in. Unfortunately, Anna and her family experienced paranormal activity in the house every single day they lived there. Sounds of footsteps could be heard above the bedroom, each step clicking as if the walker had claws. The basement was another source of spookiness. The family dog would stand guard at the top of the basement stairs and growl fiercely, the hair on its back puffed up in hackles.

Other residents of the Fort Russell house over the years have backed up its haunted reputation. The young nephew of a pair of renters saw a spirit he called George the day

they moved in. The new renters soon witnessed George for themselves. The specter wore a blue military-style uniform but quickly vanished when gazed upon. To get around the problem, they put mirrors up all through the house. The idea was to be able to see the ghost without looking directly at George and cause him to vanish. It worked, and mirrors caught George's reflection many times. No one knows who George once was. Pieces of tombstone were found below the house in the crawl space. But no writing could be seen on them.

Not all old houses can be moved or restored, even historic ones like the Draper House. In the 1880s when it was built, the large grand home shared the street with the stately manors of

Cheyenne's founding fathers. George Draper got rich during the Dakotas gold rush of the 1870s. He didn't find gold ore, but his hardware store sold tools and supplies to the gold-fevered masses. Draper was a wealthy, influential citizen who served in the territorial legislature. Fancy parties and dances attended by the town's upper class took place at the luxurious residence. And the house served as the governor's mansion during William Richards's 1895–1899 term in office.

Cheyenne and its neighborhoods changed throughout the twentieth century. By 2003, the once-stately Draper House was declared beyond repair and scheduled for demolition. Next to the abandoned home was an office building where two women worked. Neither woman knew that the other shared her same secret. On multiple occasions, both had seen someone in the second-floor window. A woman in an old-fashioned dress made of colorful fabric sat brushing her long dark hair. Both office workers say she looked down from the window at them and smiled. When shown an old archived photograph of Mrs. Draper on the home's porch, both women recognized her face. This was indeed the same person who sat in the window brushing her hair—the spirit of Mrs. Draper!

One of the women felt a particular connection to the specter and toured the condemned home. When she entered the

second-floor room, the chair by the window had a deep depression in its seat. It was as if at that very moment something unseen sat there. Both of the office workers watched the Draper House being torn down. They claim that Mrs. Draper appeared in the window a final time, lifted her arm, and waved them farewell.

# Theatre of the Macabre

Winters on the windswept Wyoming prairie can be brutally long, cold, and dark. What did people do for fun back before television, video games, movies, or even radio was around? Theaters of all sorts took up the task of entertaining those on frontier. Early versions weren't much more than tents that featured lantern slide shows that projected images on glass lit by a lantern onto a canvas screen.

As Cheyenne grew, theaters became more permanent entertainment venues.

On the site of another of the city's disasters—the collapse of two downtown buildings in 1879—a new structure was erected in 1887. It became the Atlas Theatre which still stands today. A teashop that sold candies and treats made on site was an early business in the building, as well as upstairs offices. A renovation in 1907 turned it into a true entertainment space, the Atlas Theatre. A large penny arcade filled the lobby—coin-operated machine fortunetellers, strength testers (swing the mallet and see how far up the puck goes), funhouse mirrors that distorted onlookers' reflections, and other attractions. Its soda parlor with marble counters and shining fixtures was said to be the fanciest in all the West.

The theater itself had seats for more than five hundred guests. On opening night, performers presented a bawdy burlesque act and *Why He Reformed*, a comedy. The theater's shows changed with the times, from variety vaudeville shows that featured slapstick comedians, ventriloquists, and plate spinners to silent and talking movies. Today the theater is owned by Cheyenne Little Theatre, a group that puts on old-fashioned live melodramas with audience participation. Ticket holders boo a top-hatted, mustachioed villain who ties a damsel in distress to the train tracks and then cheer loudly when the hero rescues her in the nick of time.

Actors, workers, and visitors to the Atlas Theatre have experienced drama of a different sort over the years. There are believed to be at least seven ghosts haunting the building. Paranormal incidents and sightings go back

decades. Thirty years ago, two young boys tagged along with their dads who'd come to prepare for a charity auction in the theater. The kids were running around on the empty stage when they noticed a man and a woman up in the projection room at the back of the theater. The man wore a formal suit and the woman a floor-length gown. The boys ran to tell their fathers about the couple, but when they checked the projection room, no one was there. The men said no one else was in the building.

Actor members of the theater group that performs there claim to regularly see a ghost they call the blue girl. The scent of flowers  accompanies her sightings. One actor felt a presence and thought someone had walked up beside him. When he turned to greet the person, no one was there. But a floral fragrance filled the air. An actress changing costume in a restroom became trapped when the lights went out. Assuming the old building had lost electricity, she fumbled around until her hand wrapped around the doorknob. She pulled and twisted as hard as she could, but the door refused to budge, trapping her inside. Finally the door simply opened. She ran to the stage to help, but the lights had remained on in the rest of the theater. No one had left the stage the entire time she was trapped.

The most famous ghost story related to the Atlas Theatre is also its saddest. It's a tale of an actor and actress whose careers and shared romance ended in tragedy. The stage actor played an evil villain determined to do harm to a beautiful heroine played by the actress. In real life, the pair were a romantic couple and engaged to marry. On day, the actor fell into a horrific jealous rage and shot his beloved through her heart. What brought on this violent attack is unknown. She collapsed and died. The actor then took his own life, his body later found on stage dangling from a noose made of curtain ropes. A number of people report seeing a lovely woman dressed in a flowing white gown throughout the theater. So clear is her image that she's been mistaken for a living person when first spotted. The murdering actor has also appeared, appropriately costumed in top hat and cape like the villain he played and lurking in the backstage shadows.

In 2012, a team from the Paranormal Hunting Observation Group (PHOG) investigated the Atlas Theatre for paranormal activity. They weren't disappointed. On the second floor, where the murder happened, the group recorded a bloodcurdling scream. A PHOG member called out, "If you are here, please knock!" Knocking sounds followed. When asking the spirit its name, Mitchell was heard three times. Could this have been the actress's last name or the name of the murderer? While recording with infrared cameras that work in the dark, the group captured video of a large orb, or ball of light. The orb flew out of one investigator's back just as he was finishing up saying a prayer in Latin. The group heard a voice say "Amen" at the same moment.

# Spooky Secret Societies

Cheyenne became a city in 1867, two years after the American Civil War ended. The United States was undergoing big changes at the time. Enslaved Black people became free citizens, and native peoples were losing the land their diminished communities called home for generations. New railroad lines and steam-engine trains opened up the West to opportunity-seeking immigrants and land-hungry Easterners. Starting over in a distant country, new state, or even a different town is never easy. Imagine managing it without the internet or Google. How do you find what you need? What are the rules there? Who can be trusted in business, trade, or farming? Reliable information was hard to come by, especially for those who didn't read English or lived in remote settings.

Lack of a support network of extended family or longtime friends and neighbors doomed many newcomers. Bad weather ruined farms, rustlers ended ranches, and fires closed businesses forever. Going it alone is hard. One answer was to create "mutual aid"  groups whose members helped each other. Fraternal orders like the Freemasons, Knights of Columbus, Odd Fellows, Elks, and Shriners filled a need.

They acted as insurance policies, providing members with funds to rebuild after fires or floods. Members also helped each other get jobs or find business opportunities.

At their peak, between the late nineteenth and first part of the twentieth centuries, it's estimated that as many as two out of every five adult American men belonged to at least one fraternal order. Many fraternal organizations and orders were (and are) secret societies. Secret in what way? Membership is sometimes a secret. Not all races, religions, or sexes are allowed to join. And often the rules, documents, rituals, and ceremonies of the group are only known by its members.

The Knights of Pythias is a nationwide fraternal order that professes to follow the three principles of friendship, charity, and benevolence. Cheyenne's Knights of Pythias Order No. 122 has met in the same lodge for nearly 140 years. The 1884 building is on the National Register of Historic Places. It doesn't look like much from the outside. There's a flea market shop on the street level, but an outside door leads to a long, steep, dimly lit staircase. An entrance at the top goes into a stunningly elaborate meeting room—the main hall. The high ceiling is covered in gleaming white copper tiles trimmed with gold, and the padded benches of curved wood line the walls. A dark stage dominates the hall. Heavy curtains cover its back wall, and two Knights of Pythias banners flank a podium. The throne-like chair on the stage looks like something from a past era.

Behind the stage curtains are props for ceremonies, and the floor features several small trapdoors. Mike, one of the building's trustees, uncovered a hidden trapdoor while cleaning the floor. A section of floor sagged a bit when leaned on, and he realized it was a door. Once Mike figured out how to open it, he crawled through the small doorway. It led down underneath the stage. Mike made a shocking discovery—an old casket.

Long-standing Knights of Pythias members gathered to unseal it. Inside was the decayed body of a teenage girl. She'd been in the casket for nearly five decades. Her remains went to a local funeral home, but the casket is still at the lodge. None of the fraternity members claim to know anything about the casket, the dead teen girl, or why she was buried beneath their stage. Her identity is a continuing mystery, or perhaps long-lost secret.

People regularly report strange happenings in the hallway that connects to one side of the lodge's stage. Sounds of footsteps, growling, moaning, whistles, and other odd noises are heard, as well as a padlock that rattles without being touched. A paranormal investigator heard footsteps in the hallway and then felt an invisible someone brush past him. Sound recordings of footsteps and voices while the building is empty have been made, too, as well as videos that show orbs, streaks of lights, and a shadowy silhouetted figure at the top of the stairs.

In 2010, a member of the Paranormal Investigation Team Wyoming (PITW) group returned to the lodge after midnight to retrieve a forgotten laptop. After climbing the stairs and entering, he heard a loud conversation coming from the lodge's kitchen. Yelling out greetings, he approached the kitchen as the sound of footsteps faded. No one was in the kitchen, and he gathered up his laptop and left. Cold spots and temperature drops often accompany spirit activity, according to paranormal investigators. PITW members used a temperature probe to record cold spots in the lodge's main hall, including a thirty-six-degree drop that happened in seconds.

A charity fundraiser event that capitalizes on the spooky reputation of the Knights of Pythias building is their annual "Nightmare on 17th Street" haunted house. On weekends every October for the past thirty years, a few thousand visitors tour Rooms of Horror set up throughout the building's basement. While costumed actors and spooky sets cause most of the scares, those that work the event report strange happenings they *didn't* create. Everything from doors opening and shutting on their own and batteries that won't hold a charge to the smell of pipe smoke and sightings of a shadowy figure.

Adjacent and nearby buildings hint at being haunted, too. People who work and live in them tell stories of strange unexplainable sounds at night that wake up sleepers and make dog growls at invisible intruders. One woman claims something extraordinary happened when she snapped an instant Polaroid photograph of a teenaged girl. As they watched the photo develop, a shockingly clear image appeared: a man in an old-fashioned zoot suit hovering in the air above the teen.

Some suspect a psychic medium is to blame for bringing together such a grand gathering of ghosts and spirits into one place. A newspaper from 1912 features an advertisement for a new business opening in the Knights of Pythias building. It promotes "the celebrated trance medium and scientist palmist" Madame Winterroth. Perhaps the spirits she spoke with decided to stay.

# Entombed in Stone

A church might seem like an odd place to harbor spirits from the beyond. But Cheyenne's most famous ghost story centers around St. Mark's Episcopal Church. The church is nearly as old as Cheyenne itself.

Finding "the wickedness unimaginable and appalling" in the town's rowdy, ramshackle winter railroad camp, the Reverend Joseph Cook organized St. Mark's parish in early 1868.

By autumn, he'd managed to have a church built. St. Mark's growing congregation decided to add some space and gravitas to the building in 1886. The plan was to add a stone tower in the British Gothic style of architecture: A castle-like touch of old England on the windswept Wyoming prairie. This design called for a kind of skilled stonework, or masonry, that local masons were unfamiliar with however. Luckily, the church found two new emigrants from Sweden trained in the type of masonry they wanted. Unfortunately neither spoke English yet.

Construction went well despite the language barrier. The men shaped the red-tinted Colorado-quarried lava stone into lovely arched windows and decorative mantels. The tower's base rose to forty feet in height, and the stonemasons would soon begin constructing its stately steeple. But that never happened. One day, only a single Swedish stonemason showed up for work. The second Swede couldn't communicate the cause of his coworker's absence. However, he seemed strangely nervous. The next day, neither stonemason came to the church. Nor were either ever seen again. Both had vanished from Cheyenne.

Unable to find someone able to construct a steeple, the church simply put a roof over the unfinished tower. The original steepled tower plans were shelved for the time being and the ground level area made into a private study. The church's rector at the time, George Rafter, said he often heard sounds of hammering and human chatter within the tower. It made him uncomfortable enough to abandon the study, and a pipe organ eventually took the room's place.

The plan to add a bell tower instead of a steeple started in 1927. Workers added on another twenty feet of stone tower, bringing it to sixty feet in height. They installed eleven bells weighing nearly twenty tons inside it. Construction didn't go quickly and had to be stopped several times.

Why? Workers complained about a ghost, believing it might turn violent if angered. To please the ghost, workers built it a private room inside the tower. They finished the room like any other, laying flooring, plastering the walls, and even hanging up a chandelier. The room's only entrance—and exit—is far below. Behind a special door in the church basement is an eighty-five-foot-high spiral staircase that leads to the sealed room.

In 1966, a man in a Denver nursing home asked the reverend of St. Mark's to visit him. They man told Rev. Eugene Todd that he'd known the Swedish stonemason who'd seemed nervous the day his coworker didn't show up for work. (Some accounts of the story say he *was* that hundred-year-old stonemason.) He explained that the absentee mason had slipped and fatally fallen inside the tower. Afraid of going to jail or being thrown out of the country, the Swede panicked. He stuffed the dead stonemason into an unfinished wall and closed it up with cement. For eighty years, an unknown corpse had lain entombed in the tower.

A decade or so later, the church opened the bell tower for tours. Fifty cents bought the brave access to the staircase that begins in the basement and ends under the bell chamber in the ghost's private room. One Halloween during this time, a local radio DJ and a popular psychic named Lou Wright decided to do a live radio broadcast from inside the ghost's room. Once locked in that All Hallows' Eve, psychic Wright reported sensing a frightened, upset spirit as well as the second spirit of an elderly man who used a cane. (Thought to be George Rafter, the original user of the tower as a study.) Looking out the room's window, Wright saw balls of dancing white light outside the church. The bells above them began ringing all by themselves, and a blue light began climbing up the stairs toward them. Wright claimed a slimy substance oozed from the room's baseboards and a man's voice shouted, "Get out of here while you still have your mind!"

Having gotten more excitement than he'd bargained for, the DJ called for help. Soon both

he and Wright descended the stairs and exited the church. Twenty minutes later, St. Mark's bells began ringing on their own once again. Police search the building and the surrounding area without finding evidence of Halloween tricksters pulling a prank. They did discover

an unknown white dusty substance on the room's floor.

Tours are no longer offered at St. Mark's Episcopal Church, and the tower stairs are boarded off—too unstable, say officials. But locals says they still hear voices coming from the tower and that the light turn off and on for no reason. Neighbors claim the organ plays in the middle of the night, too.

# Ghosts on the Range

The capital of Wyoming is far from the state's geographic center. In fact, Yellowstone National Park in the state's northwest corner is more than five hundred miles from Cheyenne. On the other hand, Colorado lies just a few miles down the road. Near the border between the two squarish similarly sized states is the nearly hundred-and-forty-year-old Terry Ranch.

A famous man from Wyoming's early history purchased the ranch in 1885. Francis Warren was the last territorial governor and the first state governor of Wyoming. Warren raised cattle, sheep, and sheepdogs at the Terry Ranch. His livestock company was one of many businesses and investments that made Warren into a wealthy man. By 1909, he was the richest of all Wyomingites (as they're called). Pretty good for someone who arrived in the territory at the age of twenty-three with less than a dollar in his pocket. Warren went on to serve in the US Senate for thirty-five years. During those decades, he hosted President Theodore "Teddy" Roosevelt at the Terry Ranch twice.

The Warren family and their ranch hands were far from the first humans to spend time on this land. The Cheyenne Archeology Association dug up much earlier history during an excavation at the ranch in

1964. Archeologists uncovered hundreds of arrowheads, pottery pieces, and other evidence that at least three different Native American tribes had lived or traveled through there. Artifacts from early European explorers, fur traders, gold seekers, and settlers were discovered as well.

Today, it's called Terry Bison Ranch. It's an Old West tourist attraction as well as a working bison ranch. More than twenty-five hundred American bison, or buffalo, graze the ranch's pasture. That's more bison than even existed back in Teddy Roosevelt's day. By then the vast herds of roaming bison that once numbered in the tens of millions had been hunted to near extinction. Hunters slaughtered the large hoofed animals in the late 1800s for sport and to purposefully starve out the Native Americans who depended on bison for survival. Communities of Indigenous people and bison herds were removed so the West could be opened to railroads, ranchers, farmers, and settlers.

It's no surprise that a site with so many centuries of human history would generate some ghost tales and spooky stories. The Terry Ranch is full of them—from slain cowboy card cheats to revengeful spirits of unknown origin. Employees and visitors to the ranch have reported so many sorts of strange spirit activity that Cheyenne Paranormal Investigations (CPI) came and searched for ghostly clues in five different ranch buildings.

The ranch's bunkhouse is a hotspot of suspected paranormal incidents. Built in the early 1900s for wranglers and cowboys, the two-story building now welcomes guests seeking a real ranch-hand experience. The rooms are dorm-like, with shared bathrooms, living areas, and a common kitchen. According to locals, two cowboys tussled while playing cards on the second floor. One cowboy accused the other of cheating, tempers flared, a fight caught flame, and it ended in one man's murder.

To this day, bunkhouse occupants report hearing arguing voices upstairs where the murder took place and stomping footsteps on the staircase when no one is on the second floor. Most occurrences happen between two and three o'clock in the morning, including

objects moving through the air as if tossed by an invisible hand. Guests claim their blankets have flown off of them while in bed. One man reported an invisible cat or other creature walking across his body, and lights also switch on and off by themselves. Nearby witnesses have also claimed to see someone looking out from the bunkhouse windows with the curtains pulled aside when the building is empty.

One evening during a blizzard, the ranch manager and a worker took shelter from the

whirling snow in the empty bunkhouse. After crashing on sofas in the living area, the men were ripped from sleep by noisy chattering voices and loud pounding bootsteps. Then the lights went crazy, turning off and on. After frantically searching for—and not finding—a source of the commotion, they abandoned the bunkhouse. The men preferred to battle the storm rather than unhappy spirits. A member of CPI heard knocking on the second floor of the bunkhouse during its investigation,

and when trying to enter one of the upstairs bedrooms, an invisible someone pushed him. Others heard and recorded whispering in the room and also unexplainedly smelled sweet tobacco.

Hungry visitors have a couple of eating options at Terry Ranch. But none is finer than Senator's Steakhouse. Guests can order a wide variety of items, including many bison meat cuts. Besides bison steaks, the menu offers bison short ribs, bison burgers, bison chili, bison meatloaf, and even chicken-fried bison steak. Diners might even get to meet Charlie, the ornery ghost named by restaurant workers. Besides turning on lights and flipping over chairs after lockup, the smell of cigars and coffee has been reported long after the kitchen is closed. The pesky spirit is often heard clomping up and down stairs and back and forth along the length of the building during dining hours, too.

Other prank-like incidents blamed on Charlie include banging bathroom stall doors and women being trapped in the restroom even through there's no lock on the door. Apparently the door keeps getting stuck even after the doorknob was swapped out. The bar staff claim a ball of bright blue light descended the staircase one night during cleanup after the restaurant closed. The blue light appeared to explode and was so bright that the employees were left seeing spots, like when a camera flash pops in the dark.

One bartender had a wine glass suddenly fly over his head and smash into the counter behind him. The guest he was pouring a drink for exclaimed, "Where did that come from?" The bartender blamed Charlie or one of the other resident ghosts, saying that the bartenders often feel something brush against their legs or someone tapping on their shoulders. And that recently a black floating object appeared at knee level. The somewhat spiderweb-looking thing floated along for about twelve feet before vanishing.

A less trouble-making spirit that employees and guests regularly spot around Terry Ranch appears as a small girl. A worker reported seeing a young girl standing in the kitchen hours before breakfast time. The manager claims to have seen her on the security camera monitor but not on its recording. The little girl ghost has also been sighted at one of the ranch's spookiest spots—the old giant cellar. Built in 1910, the cellar is a three-story underground structure built into a hillside. The ranch uses it to store food and other items that need to stay cool.

The small girl specter is only one of many unexplained sights and sounds witnessed in the cellar over the years. CPI experienced a whole series of strange events while investigating the lowest level of the century-old cellar. The team shivered as the temperature where they stood suddenly dropped twenty degrees for no reason. Paranormal investigators claim when a spirit is making itself present it sucks the heat energy from its surroundings, causing the chill felt by ghost hunters. While in the cellar, CPI members also had camera and recorder batteries go suddenly dead, heard voices speaking in another language, saw huge magnetic field fluctuations on their instruments, and recorded a ringing bell and human cough sound that had no source. The person operating the video camera kept trying

to film one particularly creepy corner of the cellar. But once the camera was aimed at the corner, it immediately lost focus. It was as if something stood between the camera and the cellar corner. Now that's spooky!

# Conclusion

Cheyenne has packed a lot of history into its century-plus lifespan. It quickly went from a wind-swept western territory camp of railroad workers to the capital of the new state of Wyoming. Being a central stop on a continent-connecting rail line brought all kinds to the young city: gold seekers heading north, immigrants seeking opportunity, Easterners hoping for land, cowboys drawn to wide open spaces, and more than a few crooks and outlaws. Cheyenne, Wyoming, is proud of its rootin'-tootin,' rough and rowdy Old West roots—ghosts and all.

**Mary Kay Carson** is an author of books for young people about wildlife, space, weather, nature, and history. Her books have received more than a dozen starred reviews, as well as multiple awards, including the 2019 AAAS/Subaru SB&F Prize for *Alexander Graham Bell for Kids*. She's written six titles in the Scientists in the Field series, including *The Bat Scientists*, an ALA Notable Children's Book, and *The Tornado Scientist*, an Ohio Choose To Read title. www.marykaycarson.com

Check out some of the other Spooky America titles available now!

Spooky America was adapted from the creeptastic Haunted America series for adults. Haunted America explores historical haunts in cities and regions across America. Each book chronicles both the widely known and less-familiar history behind local ghosts and other unexplained mysteries. Here's more from *Haunted Cheyenne* author Jill Pope:

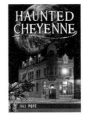